SPECIAL BRANDS
OF THE DÉJÀ VU

SPECIAL BRANDS OF THE DÉJÀ VU

Poems by
Duane A. Partain

LUMINARE PRESS
WWW.LUMINAREPRESS.COM

Special Brands of the Déjà Vu: Poems by Duane A. Partain
Copyright © 2024 by Duane A. Partain

All rights reserved. This book or any portion thereof may not be reproduced or used in any manner whatsoever without the express written permission of the publisher, except for the use of brief quotations in a book review.

Printed in the United States of America

Luminare Press
442 Charnelton St.
Eugene, OR 97401
www.luminarepress.com

LCCN: 2024909940
ISBN: 979-8-88679-576-9

*Thanks to all those I met along the way
and most of all to my wife, Jane,
for her support, loyalty, and love.*

Contents

Note .... *ix*
Foreword *1*

THERE 5
AT THE LIMA POSTE 7
THE BOOKFINDER 9
THE FISHERMAN 10
CHRISTMAS AWAY FROM HOME 13
I REMEMBER 15
QUINES CREEK ROAD 17
MOVING BLUES AGAIN 19
A FIREFLY NIGHT IN OLD CHACTÚN 20
TIMBUKTU 23
THE BATHS AT VIRGIN GORDA 25
THEY LEFT LAST WEEK 27
PONTIACS TURN ME ON 29
POST COITAL BLUES 30
TURKISH TIME 33
VIA A NUDE PHOTO 35
MOTHERS DANCE ALL NIGHT, TOO 36
PERMISSION DENIED 39

MODERN POETRY	41
REGARDING WHAT IS: A MEDITATION	42
LOVE POEM	44
TWO A.M. AGAIN	47
AN ODE TO STOLEN MOMENTS	49
PEACEFUL SOLITUDE	51
SOLITARY	53
LADYLIKE	55
WILL WINTER KILL THE CATS?	57
A HISTORY LESSON	58
PRIVATE THOUGHTS	61
ANALOG GUY IN A DIGITAL WORLD	63
RISING ALONE ANOTHER MORNING	64
UNFINISHED WORDS	67
CANADIAN VISITORS	69
THE CIRCUS IS JUST ACROSS THE RIVER	70
JEKYLL AND HYDE	73
PRIESTESSES DON'T SLEEP	75
THE QUALITY OF LIGHT WHEN FLYFISHING	77
RAIN CHASED THE FINCHES AWAY	79
LIGHT	81
OLD HOTEL	83
THE BOOTMAKER	84

PRECONCEIVED IDEOLOGY	87
EINSTEIN'S NIECE	89
NAKED BOY	91
THE VOYEUR	93
TODAY I WOKE UP DEAD	94
YELLOW DOG	97
ONCE UPON A TIME	99
WHAT DO YOU SAY TO SOMEONE DYING?	100
LAKE ANTIGUA	103
THE DAY AFTER	105
BADEN BADEN	107
THE MEXICAN BUTCHER SHOP	109
THE END OF HOLIDAYS	110
BOREDOM IS AS BOREDOM DOES	112
YOUR NAME	114
SPECIAL BRANDS OF THE 'DÉJÀ VU'	116

Note

Some of these poems were previously published in magazines and collections. These include:

"Moving Blues Again" in Alura, Volume x, Number 2, 1985

"I Remember" and "The Day After" in Alura, Volume X, Number 3, 1985

"The Rain Chased the Finches Away" and "The Fisherman" in Bird Verse Portfolio, Series 1, Number 7, 1984

"The Quality of Light When Flyfishing" in Fall Poetry, Poetry Today, 1984

"Two A.M. Again" in Songs For All Seasons, 1985

Foreword

Many people keep journals and diaries, and write letters. Some write memoirs, biographies, essays, histories, mysteries, novels, non-fiction, or science fiction. And many people also try their hand at writing poetry.

Several of my articles, short stories, and poems have been published in newspapers, magazines, and collections. Many of these writings chronicle my life working in the hospitality and culinary industry. I have lived and worked in five countries, ten states, and had over twenty different jobs. Moving often and traveling the world has brought me in contact with interesting people, wonderful sights, and unusual experiences, often offering the spark of a poem.

"Poetry and Science are both manifestations of the spirit that creates new ways of thinking of the world, in order to understand it better," says the physicist and writer, Carlo Rovelli.

And from the poet, Dylan Thomas, "A good poem is a contribution to reality…and helps us to extend everyone's knowledge of himself and the world around him."

Poetry comes in many forms: limerick, ode, sonnet, haiku, hip-hop, nursery rhymes, free verse, songs, rap, blues, and rock & roll to name a few. When reading or hearing poetry I've often wondered where that thought, that comparison, that idea, that line came from. So I've decided to share a brief description of the inspiration or origin of the poems in this book.

My poetry is narrative, I think. There is a small story, an image, a description, a situation, a place, a time, a person in each of the poems. One idea, one thought, one circumstance, one event, one emotion, one experience per poem.

The following pages bring out various pieces of my life along with a bit of background information on each poem to help the reader understand what prompted the poem. Some origins are obvious; some less so. The poems are not chronological, but each one comes authentically from my experience.

Reading poetry out loud is a great way to really hear what the poet intended. Perhaps as you read, you will be inspired to write your own poetry.

—DUANE PARTAIN

Special Brands of the Déjà Vu

Poems by
Duane A. Partain

THERE

I grew up there amid farms, fields, norms;
where machines, people, winds tilled the soil.
Close by were mountains, rivers, earth shapes.
The far off was lights, city sounds, concrete trees.

I grew up there in the streets, buildings, towers
where books, ideas, thoughts were valued.
Close by were derelicts, ruins, abandoned spaces.
The far off was exotic, fanciful, a vision.

I grew up there, new places, new tastes, new realities
where colors, views, landscapes differed.
Close by were unknowns, strangers, and myths.
The far off was the world waiting, inviting, impatient.

I grew up there wandering, traveling, asking—
where the past, the present, the future twined.
Close by was the new, the old, the present—all combined.
The far off is here where I am now—this place.
   I grew up there.

*Our lives are the sum of our experiences in different places.

AT THE LIMA POSTE

Languid against one wall, a hook-nosed Inca maiden
Graced the space underneath the vaulted roof
Instantly transforming the heavy, hanging beams
Into a soaring fortress rivalling fabled Machu Picchu.

Timeless amidst the coppered masses
Her dusky eyes bore into my gringo-ness
Illiterally reading me perfectly, she laughed
as I turned away, hiding my lust behind a solitary
   postcard.

**Travel enriches. Peru has many fabulous sights and this
brief encounter.*

THE BOOKFINDER

The Bookfinder came today
and cleared shelves
of pamphlets, posters, books, and plays.
"I buy whatever sells," he says.
He carried albums, ephemera, and maps away.

The Bookfinder came today
looking for histories, photos,
journals, letters, calendars, emptied trays
of newspapers, articles, cards, and memories.
He trundled full boxes and sacks away.

The Bookfinder came today
collecting plans and hopes and dreams
in diaries, old school papers, ragged pages,
and a stack of incomplete poems.

The Bookfinder came today.
He took the unfinished stuff away
my life's parts gone in just one day
when the Bookfinder came today.

*Every community has tradesmen with unusual occupations.

THE FISHERMAN

A heron hunches up against Fall's first cold wind
watching the water rushing 'round river's bend.

Waiting for a fly carried on a floating leaf
he stands bent, cocked angularly like a broken reed.

Craned neck, motionless, intently searching for a careless fish
one foot tucked, half-hidden by swirling fog and mists.

Blackened dock pilings poke their heads like rows of choreographed seals
watching the great, blue bird look for his afternoon meal.

As he moves closer to shore does he seek the comfort of land?
Is he listening for instructions from cattails or reading hieroglyphics in the sand?

Leaving twice, rising slowly to glide quietly away
he dries his long gun-metal wings in the sun's
   waning rays.

Now silhouetted, a feathered snag against the skyline
patient and stately—the old fisherman.

Herons look ungainly until they fly.

CHRISTMAS AWAY FROM HOME

Hair all white with a beard and a belly
clutching a glass of Scotch
in a trailer court in Mexico at Christmas time.

Playing Santa in the afternoon heat, handing treats
to little children in rags.
Crying and raging, he tried to help them all.

"No wife, all alone, my one son,
my claim to fame—
on TV—the 'Man from Glad'—I'm his dad!"

*In Mexico, alone at the holidays, his emotions got the better of him. Santa broke character.

I REMEMBER

I remember when my father told of growing up
    in Hungry Hollow, just down from Mount
    Magazine;
Coon dogs whose singing sound on a clear Ozark night
    carried all of three counties;
Grandpa shooting a stump, after drinking too much,
    the five bullet holes covered by a single silver dollar.

Visiting there on a Fall day last year
    a turkey gobbled like in a Faulkner story.
The campfire smoke caught in the red oak leaves
    stayed, lying in the air for three days.
We stopped at a dirt floor store with chickens in boxes
    and cold beer in a battered old Coke machine.

Peeing in the woods was fun for me; for him
    it was shameful, being dirt poor.
Those southern mountains and selected memories
    are stories richly told.
Now fireflies, loblolly pines, and the soft drawl,
    "Y'all come back, ya hear," I remember too.

*All of our relatives tell "old times" stories. I visited the area they talked about.

QUINES CREEK ROAD

Often I wanted to slow down, turn, and drive up
  Quines Creek Road
eyeing the long, grey line leading through the woods
    wondering who lived at its end and why.
Who would move there far from home, away from
  friends?
Are they old and lonesome or a young couple who
  scrimshaw together?
Did they one day leave Detroit to grow garlic and
  raise watch geese
or come to photograph Fall's reflection in the streams
  and stayed on?
Do these mysterious ones stand in silence and awe
  of first growth firs
or plot to hew and build their dream on the
  mountainside?
Often I wanted to slow down, turn, and drive up
  Quines Creek Road.
But I never did. Only looked up, wondered, and
  drove quickly by.

** On every drive, we pass road signs to other places. I still
intend to take this turnoff one day.*

MOVING BLUES AGAIN

The old house has already changed
with blankets and lamps, I'm moving again.
"It smells of you," a friend once said,
"the muskiness here is your scent."

That wafting by, was it old lady Ruby
whose letters come here still?
Or odor of occupant lingering
in the dust-filled air?

A bent man, Mills, lived here
the clumps of grasses say.
He planted roses and apple trees.
His is a musty, an earthy smell.

Will someone say they knew me
by what their senses glean on moving day?
Or will I leave nothing, known only to spiders,
whiffs of wind and the grey cat in the alley.

*I've lived and worked in 10 states and 5 countries, moving at least 20 times.

A FIREFLY NIGHT IN OLD CHACTÚN

Jungle grew over Chactún; tall stelae staring;
half covered ruins, broken steps, abandoned
   temples and towers;
hot damp air, humidity of the long dead hanging
   in the stillness.
Sherds that once held life's necessities
strewn about by a careless hand were curiosities now.
Tombs were there, I know, buried deep, overgrown,
where treasures lay in vaults guarded by scorpions.
Old white roads, "sacbeob," lead to other forgotten cities.
Pre-history it is called because no one wrote then,
but their calendars knew of time
four thousand years into the past.
One day they—whoever they were—walked away
leaving the giant stone columns with no one to talk to.

Deep, deep in old Mexico, Chactún it was, with a girl
who had long blonde hair and watched for bats in
   the firefly night.
We shared a sweaty love, afraid of snakes and the dark
daring each other to admit it wasn't fun.

**A six month trip deep into Mexico and Central America
brought me to ancient Aztec, Maya, Olmec, Zapotec, Mixtec
ruins and descendants…civilizations covered in jungle growth
and mystery are wonderful sights. It was a once-in-a-lifetime
experience. Many areas where I camped are now covered
with resort hotels. Others are pockets of deepest poverty.*

TIMBUKTU

"The meeting place of all who travel by camel or canoe."☙
Where Saharan sands and Niger water leads you to
that land of poems, a desert oasis, a place of old
    where nothing's new—
a marketplace of salt, of gold, of illuminated
    manuscripts—it's true!

Merchants, soothsayers, scribes, scholars too,
royalty, priests, and the curious—to name a few.
All travel there to visit, to trade, to pray, to muse.
A worldly, wondrous, motley crew.

So far from all the legends, the tales, the mysteries grew
to fill the hearts, the minds, the books of those who knew
of its sparkling treasures, its peoples' hues,
    magnificent mosques and marvelous views.
I've seen Bagan; I loved Peru; but I'm sorry I never got
    to Timbuktu.

☙ *from a Sudanese chronicle; a desert saying*
**A fabled, historical desert city which called to me my entire life. Alas, I never got to see it for myself.*

THE BATHS AT VIRGIN GORDA

Carolina's boulders lie in the Caribbean,
rolled there by Pleistocene gougings
leaving the noble granite giants stranded;

to be splashed on by idled, leisured masses
who play in the shaded grottos, climbing,
treating them like toys, too casually.

**Once I interviewed for a job in the Caribbean. The large
granite boulders at Virgin Gorda have been compared to the
ones off the Carolina coast thirteen hundred miles away.*

THEY LEFT LAST WEEK

Three sugar maples in the back yard
served as bases in the Summer time
for games of ball or hide and seek.
Lord, they had some barbeques there!

But now it's unkempt, weedy, mossy—an idle lawn.
At the edges ferns and bushes grow
where croquet pegs and horseshoes
rang among the family sounds.

The rooms are empty, no laughter,
no slippered feet on carpet runners.
Silent hallways lead past crumpled left-behinds
to doors where cobwebs hang.

It stands forlorn that house
where children yelled and ran and fought.
Now only sunlight shafts and shadows
dance and play, crying to be let out.

Everywhere there are empty buildings where people once lived.

PONTIACS TURN ME ON

Smooth, powerful, a sleek machine.
Inside leather soft, heat on high.
Rain outside, windows fogged.
Clothes everywhere.
Suzy showed me how.
Do you have to ask why Pontiacs turn me on?

A first sexual experience…

POST COITAL BLUES

Afterwards, she wants a cigarette, I would rather
 fall asleep.
We talk of books just read, I trace her body line
 toe to hair.
Unliberated, I touch her stretch marks and shudder.
Her nipples still erect at my touch, love making
 satisfied.
Moist bruised lips, a damp curl on her forehead.
We lie spent, curled together.

Summer outside and inside jazz tones.
We whisper soft obscenities because
"Love talk is dirty talk," Tennessee Williams writes.
The top of the Moon she says. I wish I could go.
Instead of wonderment, I wonder why.
Pondering the morality of amorality
we decide for the hundredth time not to meet again.

A quiet time, re-newed, re-robed, the world beckons.
After becomes before and "When next?" the
 breathless topic.
Fingertips along the cheek one last time.
A hair on the pillow is left.
Tea and solitary thoughts replace her smell.
Sometimes it is lonely afterwards.

*Emotions we all have, I think, often get jumbled up. Hard to know what is right.

TURKISH TIME

Dark-eyed,
Sharp-tongued,
Drunk on Raki,
Throwing her left leg over mine
Challengingly,
Willingly,
Sensually,
She became the victor, again.

*I was in the Army in Germany. She wanted to have lots of kids and learn to drive a big American car. I came home without her.

VIA A NUDE PHOTO

Apsara, you are, in myth
    coiffed, bejeweled—Hindu
Paleolithic adoration, abstract
    featureless—Moravian
Fertility symbol, realistic
    voluptuous—Neanderthal
DNA descendant, mitochondrial
    reproduced—African
Born of the Rainbow Snake—Arnhem land,
    Dreamtime—Aboriginal
A gift from the trickster Raven
    changeling—Haida
Sculpted in bas relief, pigments, clay
    a Venus celebration—universal.

Many human characteristics are shared across centuries, cultures, and continents.

MOTHERS DANCE ALL NIGHT, TOO

"Imagine my mother dancing..."
JOAN DIDEON—DEMOCRACY

Imagine your mother dancing wearing blue taffeta
at a dancehall where sweaty soldiers' arms
snake slowly down her side, feeling for the swell
of her breast, coming to rest pressing the small of
   her back.

Imagine your mother dancing in black silk stockings
seams straight up the back of her legs
meeting where the taut swell of her flanks
come together at the soldier's bulls-eye.

Imagine your mother dancing on Fridays
at the tea dance at the Hilton
with a stately, older gentleman
flirting, foxtrotting, sipping Scotch.

Imagine your mother dancing to old records,
alone in a room, turning slowly,
remembering exciting nights
when the stupor of love suffocated.

Imagine your mother dancing
on the head of a pin with a thousand angels
sharing stories of breathless, ageless, timeless love,
whirling, happily dancing the eons away.

*A line in a poem written by someone else inspired me.

PERMISSION DENIED

    I asked
but she said
      no.

*It happened several times. I wondered why?

MODERN POETRY

I don't understand modern poetry.
Pytheas didn't ever visit New York.
Often strange comparisons, odd allegories,
   obscure references,
cultural interpretations, mnemonic devices elude me.
The Songhay had poetic manuscripts, songs,
illuminations, treatises in twelfth century text.
Ululations, lamentations, eulogies known to all.

I don't understand modern poetry.
Why re-examine Frost, re-interpret Cao Cao,
   parse Zayeta?
Why re-analyze Alhazen, re-define Nagarjuna,
dissect Lucretius, question Yalatkit, re-translate Hafez?
Their tapestries do not need to be re-woven.
A grouse is a grouse; an oryx an oryx, love is love.
Not hidden meanings, not new truths, not alien proof.
No discoveries anew, no undoing of verse, no revelations.
Definitions of our time and place already handed down.

I don't understand modern poetry. Do you?

---

* Many different forms of poetry by many authors have been written, read, and enjoyed for thousands of years.

REGARDING WHAT IS: A MEDITATION

Sitting contemplating, reflecting, musing,
I realize I know nothing of the world.

Sitting laughing, thinking, crying,
I realize I know nothing of emotions.

Sitting writing, reading, talking,
I realize I know nothing of reality.

Sitting listening, daydreaming, wishing,
I realize I know nothing of desires.

Sitting chanting, singing, shouting,
I realize I understand few sounds.

Sitting smelling, tasting, drinking,
I realize I understand little of my senses.

Sitting fuming, swearing, blaspheming,
I realize, I understand I lack insight.

But sitting…simply being…
I realize and understand all.

*An article on the life of a monk was the starting point here.

LOVE POEM

When I am in love
too often I wonder
about when love ends.

I never understood
that part—the
crying and accusing.

But this time no
matter. We fit together
like two old men

who sit and
talk on benches
in the park.

Two old men
who pitch horseshoes and
know each other well.

Two old men
who meet there
though it's cold

and winds have edges
sharp enough to cut
down Autumn's last grasses.

We like each
other that well
you and I.

I don't wonder about
endings, just if forever
will be long enough.

My poem to my wife, Jane, for our wedding day

TWO A.M. AGAIN

Who do you call at two in the morning
    when you are so lonesome you could scream,
    when you want to cry but are afraid to,
    when you want to forget but can only remember?

Can you dial your ex and reminisce,
    or tell your parents it could have been better,
    or wake up an old lover to say thank you,
    or do you pour another drink and weep boozily?

Is it better to sit with your cat—just the two of you
    hoping memories will die when sleep comes,
    wanting to hold someone but not yourself,
    wishing tomorrow would come ten hours sooner?

Who do you call at two in the morning
    when life no longer creeps by but rushes past,
    when time runs out of the hour glass,
    when love is the answer but you are alone?

*We all get feeling lonely once in a while.

AN ODE TO STOLEN MOMENTS

We met but once. I knew first time
our hearts would meet, our limbs entwine.

Where we passed boughs were laden down
with weighty thoughts of love's seeds sown.

Gently we spoke of times when our hearts
would strong beat together and stop should we part.

Soft worlds of sighs, of glances forbidden
times of touching from all others hidden.

Alas, storm clouds came, found true love wanting
began the spiral toward sweet sorrows parting.

Fondnesses dwell where love boldly strode
now inhabits the mind which was Cupid's abode.

The gentle I knew in your face and your touch
were gifts from the gods and memories enough.

*An affair

PEACEFUL SOLITUDE

One day before a fireplace listening
to a Winter storm crash against the window pane
and howl its tale of sunken ships;
I wondered of men so bold and rough
who dared the sea,
reveled when the days were cold,
and shouted back obscenities.

Climbing masts with fingers numbed
by icy blasts made men of boys
and widowed strong, patient women.
That's not for me. Satisfied to sip the grape,
stoke the flame, and read of derring-do,
I would rather write these words
and wait for the warmth of you.

*A cold, windy, rainy night on the Oregon coast in front of a roaring fireplace waiting for the girl I was to marry to come home from work.

SOLITARY

Sometimes when I watch sunsets my mind identifies with skies
fragmented by odd shapes of clouds, colors that run together,
and non-patterns of light and dark.
Sometimes I think that way.

Sometimes I drive, and when freeways mirage away I think,
"That's me. Do interstates begin or end? Do my thoughts? Do I?"
Sometimes I think that way.

Sometimes I sit in hotel rooms bouncing ideas off antiseptic walls
wishing for diseases best caught by social contact.
Sometimes I think that way.

But mostly when I watch, or drive, or sit,
I think of you.

One of those kinds of moments.

LADYLIKE

The way she licked herself, gently
removing milk from her upper lip
as if anyone could do that so sensuously.

Stretching in the sun, skin glistening,
more like a machine than anything else.
Finely tuned, a special, sporty model.

Once, on a Winter walk, she bared her breasts;
daring to be ladylike in the layered midst
of sweaters, mufflers, woolen clothes.

Later, older, no less beautiful, behaving outrageously
boasting of her past, spouting poetry
and when she slept, snoring gracefully.

Observing people often leads to a poem.

WILL WINTER KILL THE CATS?

I live in a motel room.
To avoid the responsibility of house payments
I pay daily instead.

Studying to be a Doctor,
or a Biologist, or Researcher. I'm not sure.
I don't work steadily.

Hazed by such unclear visions
many nights and days and in between times,
I drink red wine copiously.

Four years from now, or ten, somewhere
at an unspecified time and place,
I hope to meet success head on.

Until then, between bills and papers,
out back, in a bowl, I put scraps
hoping this Winter won't kill the cats.

It was a long, dark, cold Winter.

A HISTORY LESSON

Yesterday I saw death tracks, an ending of a journey.
Today I hurried homeward to find embers, still smoking.
Tomorrow I should rebuild. The worry?
   Craftsmanship—my lack of it.

What has already happened dictates terms; the who,
   what, where.
Politicians speak of negotiations always in process,
but the outcome is ordained; chaos, ruin,
   degeneration—a given.

Watches run down because no one winds them.
Couples part when egos collide, trample, and run loose.
Seers, prognosticators, psychics—belches in the wind.

Lao-Tsu, Luther, Plotinus, Nostradamus—
   philosophers or madmen?
Answers in the entrails of a dog, tea leaves, or a
   confessional
all lead to ashes and dust, legends and myths.

Yesterday I saw death tracks and marveled at their delicacy.
Today I hurried homeward stopping to listen to a meadowlark.
Tomorrow I will pick up a hammer, aim carefully and begin again.

An attempt to explain the world by me, for me, to me.

PRIVATE THOUGHTS

Another day of fossicking about
roving inside walls mossy with
accumulations of soft, quiet thoughts.

Outside, chuckling to himself,
a passerby nodding in the rain,
smiling, fictionalized his life.

"Grey leaves," a poet once said,
"our lives are grey leaves."
There are Autumn's hues, but

they too become grey, falling wraith-like
to be scuffed into piles by children
and peed on by old dogs.

Pessimism is often a human response.

ANALOG GUY IN A DIGITAL WORLD

I tried to e-mail, text, call you,
but the many dots, flashing red lights,
black lines, green triangles, circles going 'round,
blue screen, white spaces, moving arrows,
bars, slides, keys got in the way.
Tiny label-less symbols, large glowing icons,
dings, bings, buzzes, tappings, small numbers,
obscure messages, unknown words, unclear
   directions,
language-less pixels, bytes, gigs, emoji, apps galore,
and only the cloud knows for sure.
But fear not; AI is coming and all will be well.
Isn't the modern world swell!? ;-)

*Thanks to Great Britain's poet, John Cooper Clarke,
for the idea and title.*

RISING ALONE ANOTHER MORNING

It's not that I mind being alone another morning;
But I know it will happen other mornings —
most other mornings.

It's not that I mind being by myself;
But I will be by myself this afternoon
and this evening.

It's not that I mind not being with someone;
But days and nights with just me
can get lonely.

It's not that I mind no one to talk to. I talk to me;
But what I have to say is best said to
one other person.

It's not that I mind rising and wondering what to do;
But I would like to feel the warmth of
someone beside me.

It's not that I mind waking and looking at grey mists;
But often I associate grey with me
and become grey.

It's not that I mind knowing I'll be alone all day;
But I wonder if it happens to others
or just to me?

It's not that I mind being alone another morning;
But I've begun to get used to it.
I don't want to.

Yet another lonely time…wondering

UNFINISHED WORDS

Today a poem just begged to be written
so I sat all day with sharp pencil, fiddlin'.
Playing with words like "sums" and "suns,"
but the sense of it all the paper shunned.
Oh for hours I wrote, erased, tried,
drank beer, watched squirrels, laughed, and cried.
Surely there must be an easier way,
someone who will tell you just what to say.
Perhaps there is no answer, no absolute truth;
maybe it is simple like gin and vermouth.
Blank pages, smudged lines add to my sorrow.
It's late, I'm weary, I'll try rhyming tomorrow.

A playful poem

CANADIAN VISITORS

Seven geese, hull down against the setting sun;
wings angled, bent, tips brushing the water.
The scene—oriental brush strokes; Zen-like
stark, dark contrasts on an orange tippled river.

For a moment even time suspends its flight
to listen to honking perfectly harmonized and watch
the formation like Corsairs, bending slowly, blending,
suspended, marionetted, fading into silhouettes.

*Geese used to leave in the winter. Now they stay the year 'round.

THE CIRCUS IS JUST ACROSS THE RIVER

All day they set up tents, sweating in the hot sun
building fantasies out of red cardboard boxes,
   unpacked trunks,
trailers, top hats, tights, erecting a monument to fun.

Dozing in the shade, animals, old hands at this game
watch jugglers practice alongside brightly painted trucks.
Trainers, showmen, acrobats all have some small
   claim to fame.

Tonight the music, carried by the hot summer's winds
is the circus for me. Costumed bears, tigers leaping,
and a troupe of sad-faced clowns supplied by just
   my mind.

Oom-pah-pahs, marches, a stately waltz, and rock
   and roll
herald the acts. Between the breezes, rustlings,
   snatches of
"Bellini and his seals"… "Look now"… and "Up there,
   high on the pole."

Imagining prancing pachyderms and trapeze
   artists soaring,
a balancing team where no one ever falls or drops a
   single spinning plate.
I hear announcements, come-ons, continuous roaring.

For hours I enjoy the sounds of the circus show
clapping for dancing horses, showgirls, and a fire eater.
Tomorrow I'll be here again, hoping the wind will blow.

*There are no more traveling circuses. The economics of such large clusters of animals, equipment, people, and PETA ended the traveling circus.

JEKYLL AND HYDE

Today I feel awkward like someone else is inside
 these clothes.
Another who holds his arms differently from me;
 I don't know these moves.

The world seems only black and white not normal
 golden colors.
Odors now are all mixed up: I can't tell one from
 the other.

The Summer sounds are different, too, alien to this
 stranger's ears.
My emotions now are jangled; my laugh is just like
 my tears.

This person is old, sickly, only talking in riddles
 and rhymes.
No one understands so he draws pictures and acts
 out a mime.

Who is this visitor here and where did the real me go?
I was here yesterday: who will be here tomorrow?

Humans all have many conflicting emotions, ideas, thoughts.

PRIESTESSES DON'T SLEEP ❧

Whenever he fell down
She helped him up.
Whenever he lost his way
She led him to the light.
Whenever he slipped,
She took command.
Whenever he blasphemed
She showed him the rites.
Whenever he pled for mercy
Her orders rang out.
Instead of crumbling unto himself
She led him to her temple.

❧ *For Chris and BB*
Anthills of the Savanna *by Chinua Achebe*

*I am often impressed by others' writings. This reflects my response to a book I read.

THE QUALITY OF LIGHT
WHEN FLYFISHING

About six fifteen in the evening on the Rogue River
   in May
the light slants orange at an angle
calculated by the gods to rest on the very top of the water.

Tall dark firs stoop at the stream's edge
and blink, wondering at their own reflections
or bending down just to see the quality of light.

* *It was a beautiful day with a gorgeous sunset on an Oregon
river the evening I wrote this.*

RAIN CHASED THE FINCHES AWAY

A flock of finches gathered on my lawn today.
They laughed and swooped and loved
with darting pecks and feathered touches.
One found a piece of yarn to soft a nest.

A dandelion stem held one tiny singing bird
no heavier than the bloom had been.
Summer came with those finches;
the sun made them golden hovering there.

They're gone now, chased away by a sudden storm.
Raindrops bathed them, became too heavy.
Yellow flashes in the grey.
I hope they come again to play.

*The bright color of finches adds joy to any garden.

LIGHT

The light out the window of the Inn
made a cross in the white snow piled deep,
bringing the eaves to eye level.
No sound at all, stillness absolute
different from grey or ivory.

Polar bears, Aleuts, weathermen
huddled in dens, igloos, beds,
live with the starkness of such white,
waiting for an end to the darkness,
waiting for the light.

*A snowy night in a Montana hotel triggered this one.

OLD HOTEL

Flowered wallpaper, once bright, hangs faded in ribbons,
falling down like a slow motion waterfall.
A dreadful sameness of hallways and bleak rooms.
Spaces full of lurching, tired, loosely wrapped souls.
Everyone is a victim, languishing, festering,
breathing air stained sickly sweet with sweaty,
   drunken laughter.
The smell is familiar; too many people; too much sorrow;
a stench of, not evil, but anger, fear, loss of hope.
Life here has a grimness which emits its own light
but provides little illumination in this dreary place.
There is no future, only a montage of herky-jerky now
where it doesn't matter how terrible the past
   might have been.
Still, in this steaming darkness of urgencies
time was less hurried than anywhere they had ever been.

An old abandoned, small-town hotel held many stories and secrets, I know. I know because every hotel I worked in was rife with intrigue, interesting people, odd happenings, and unusual situations.

THE BOOTMAKER

Cowboy boots, made
soft like socks
by hand by
old man Jesse
who measures the
ankle and feet
accounting for the
bumps and dents.
Two shopworn books
hold foot lives.
I'm there, though
only the wise,
gnarly, stained hands
of Jesse know.
Glued and sewn,
stitched like wind.

Duane A. Partain

Everyone should own
such a proof
of someone's honest
labor of love.
Gloves for feet
handmade by Jesse.

One of my many jobs was at a resort dude ranch in Arizona. I had to play the part, so I sought out a bootmaker. He was an interesting old cowboy, a story teller, and a well-respected craftsman. Once I had five pair of Jesse's handmade boots of exotic leathers. In 2022, at the Pendleton Roundup, I sold them all to a pretty cowgirl.

PRECONCEIVED IDEOLOGY

The woods were calm, the woods were dark.
A careless word set off the spark.
"What! A family new upon 'ar road!"
"But dear, after all, they're only toads."
"No mind, they're not 'ar kind and that's no good."
"But respect our neighbors, I think we should."
"Bah! We'll raise a ruckus, scream and shout,
 burn, form clans and drive 'em out.
We'll show these toads they can't get in.
Would you want a toad for one of your kin?"
And so they burned, cried out, and shouted,
 did their best and finally routed
the family of toads who went back to their logs
driven out by a band of frogs.

Obvious, eh?

EINSTEIN'S NIECE

At a friend's house once, I met Einstein's niece,
a wispish, waspish, bent-over lady, Margie.
Drinking tea we talked of Siamese cats,
of gardens ripening late that year
and bus schedules changed for no good reason.
I could have asked if he ever told her
how energy and light really mix
or explained if time did slow down in space?
But really I wanted to know if he was a kindly man,
    enjoyed a cold beer,
and if she liked her Uncle Einstein.

Across the street from a relative lived Einstein's niece.

NAKED BOY

Picasso must have painted the gaunt, sallow child
who wades at the water's edge.
Intent on floating bark and river-smoothed rocks
he winds up, throws. It skips three—no, four times.
The geyser sound is lost in the passing wind.
Crablike, he stoops to listen
or does he see pastels and watercolor hues?

A small boy skipping rocks led to this one.

THE VOYEUR

Four hours ago a supple and lovely young lass
came to lie in the sun, to toast, to bask.
Turning over, back and forth, to and fro
browning her lithe young body so.
Lying, stretching, fairly sizzling,
oiled, rubbed down, sweaty, glistening.

Should I not look, dare I not dream
of her body so young, so sensual, so lean.
Tan is now where light was then,
tight butt and breasts, my thoughts a sin.
'Twas like a ritual—a pagan Mass.
Now nothing's left but indentations in the grass.

*You know how guys are.

TODAY I WOKE UP DEAD

This morning I saw myself dead.
I woke to a mirrored image of me, prone
in a cold room, dressed in a black suit.
(I went to bed in it last night.)

Dead, I looked all right, serene, sedate,
at ease with the life acts so far played.
I didn't want to move, to interrupt the peacefulness.
For much of the day, I lay there, dead.

I could imagine people gathered 'round, remarking
on my suit, how well I looked, how natural.
The ceremonies would be nil, not liking pomp and such,
and not too much sniffling either, I hoped.

Remarks about the work I did (and didn't do)
and how I really liked to read more than sweat.
They joked a bit while eating sweets and said nice things.
No eulogies, no "how clever he was" stories.

But when the imagined talk turned to interment,
crossing the bar, and cremation, I wanted to get up—
to shout and swing my arms and laugh,
though I'm not normally such a jolly sort.

So, with a sigh, chuckling, I rose from the dead,
fed the cat, and mused on how few get the chance
to view themselves passed on and listen
to what is said about them when they are dead.

*I once lived in rooms where the closet doors all along the walls were big mirrors. One night I went out to a dinner, drank too much, wandered home, fell asleep, and woke up looking at myself in the mirrors.

YELLOW DOG

Behind the closed down tavern
by the piles of scrap and ruin
lived a yellow dog.

Among the broken boards,
under a long-abandoned car
lived a yellow dog.

Beside the sparse shrubs
nesting like a bird
lived a yellow dog.

With the passing seasons
in harshly changing weather
lived a yellow dog.

Using callings to the wind
and old, cold chicken
Now, I have a yellow dog.

*A friend adopted a dog rescued from an Indian reservation. I grew up on an Indian reservation, so I thought I knew just where the dog came from.

ONCE UPON A TIME

Once there were trees
Fire began burning them

Once there were rocks
Waters rose covering them

Once there were fish
Acids rained suffocating them

Once there were birds
Winds roared overwhelming them

Once there were animals
Climates changed killing them

Now there are no   trees
                                      rocks
                                      fish
                                      birds
                                      animals

Humans came, untutored
Ending them all

Does life go on and on and on? A poem about now…

WHAT DO YOU SAY TO SOMEONE DYING?

What do you say to someone dying?
Do you ask them to tell you their dreams
and try to decipher meanings?

Do you ask about family; why the son was jailed;
why the marriage failed?

Do you ask about feelings or let the emotions
pour out onto the floor?

Do you inquire about health, nod knowingly
about pain, suffering, and night sweats?

No. You hold them, stroke their brows,
listen to reminiscences and old stories.

No, you touch their bruises, scars, sores
and marvel at the healing of their wounds.

No, you cook, bring good pastries,
brew hot tea and sauté expensive chanterelles.

Duane A. Partain

No, you make them comfortable with soft blankets, words of great praise, your love, and read to them.

What do you say to someone dying?
Everything, something, nothing. All is perfect.

As we age, the end of life is another period of time that each of us must confront.

LAKE ANTIGUA

Two small, hand-carved, wooden toys
bargained for in all eagerness
by the gringa tourist
for her mantel back home.

"Pero, *señora*, por favor,
 if you take them
 for any price, my little girls—
 what will they play with?"

*At a large mountain lake in Guatemala in a small village,
two little girls were playing with hand-carved wooden dolls
made by their father. (Sometimes the backstory is longer
than the poem.)*

THE DAY AFTER

The day after Halloween a warm wind from the south
darted through town, willow-wispish, in and out
blowing left-over spells and potions into the void.
One lonely incantation buried
in the ankle deep fall colored leaves escaped.

For years I wondered where that spirit went
till one day I read of a lady in Phoenix
who killed her parrot, strangled two rubber trees,
and ate snails for two weeks straight.

A Halloween tale

BADEN BADEN

The Baths are why they came.
Not just to cleanse medieval dirt and grime
but evil humors chased away
by healing mineral waters.

Four hundred years of time,
and dust, and acids fill the waters
with modern, weary pilgrims.
Their bodies, look, and minds numbed the same.

The waiting waters are the draw.
Cleansed spirits pave the way
for humans to try again.
For the Baths, the world is changeless.

*A tourist destination dating from early historical times

THE MEXICAN BUTCHER SHOP

Just as raw and naked as a dog killed by a car
lying smeared all over the road,
meat hangs, strewn about in strips, chunks, and parts.

Blood sausage with real blood, and chickens with
 combs a'waving,
fish and fur and fowl lie about
at four pesos apiece, really quite a saving.

To shop for a meal, an afternoon snack, or a party
takes cultural guts. In this market
to handle these wares you have to be hearty.

So much savagery in full view and not one complaint.
Odors, flies, someone's meal to be.
Buy by the kilo, check carefully the weight.

Those counters and tiles can never be made white again,
not even by the old cleaning man
who scrubs stall to stall talking to the hog's heads.

**Markets in other countries are always colorful and
interesting opportunities to learn about the people, their
food, their customs, and their culture.*

THE END OF HOLIDAYS

The holiday address book is tattered—
Held together by tape, string, and a rubber band.

The holiday address book is worn
By time, neglect, and that great big coffee stain.

The holiday address book tells quiet stories
The blind of drama softened by time.

The holiday address book has few new entries.
Fewer people or just fewer memories?

The holiday address book pages are smudged
By many a Happy, Happy, Ho, Ho, Ho and Merry,
  Merry, Merry!

The holiday address book has many blank pages.
I didn't get their names. I should have.

The holiday address book, a history of stories,
Weddings, births, bar mitzvahs, moves, exes,
  beginnings, endings.

Duane A. Partain

The holiday address book has unknown people,
Dates and names crossed out. Who were they?

One day the holiday address books of others
Will X out and cross my name off too.

As I completed my holiday cards, it became clear to me.

BOREDOM IS AS BOREDOM DOES

I should be bored. All I've done lately is:
write a novel, take a trip, engage relatives, plant bulbs,
   do laundry, get physical therapy,
visit doctors, take long walks, grocery shop, exercise,
   cook, read dozens of books, sell exotic rugs,
pet the cat, be a good husband, nest, play cards, dream.

I should be bored. With all the time I have I could…
be an entrepreneur, start a car factory,
visit nursing homes, read to children,
hitch hike in Mexico just to see what happens,
move and build a one-room cabin in forests far away,
learn to swear in Italian or Tagalog, or
become Buddhist—or, better yet, Jewish.

I should be bored, but I'm not.
I make lists of what is yet to come.
The next poem is just around that corner.
Visions, insights, understandings live everywhere
  …waiting.

All I've done so far is/isn't all wrong/right.
Would a new life-style be really meaningful today?
About that boredom…later please. I don't have time
   right now.

* Triggered by a chance remark regarding my "retirement"

YOUR NAME

When your name is spoken for the last time
what will be said to describe your life?

Will the tales and stories be true or made of
false judgements, opinions, and your lies?

Can the intimate moments be told?
Can the history of you and all of them come alive?

When your name is spoken for the last time
what will be said of you to honor, or revile, or despise?

Will the remembrances and reminiscences
recreate the essences of your sense of style?

Can the ending be such that the reflection
of what you really were be the last entry in the final file?

When your name is spoken for the last time
will there be a shout, applause, a guffaw, a tear,

A murmur, a snort, a cry? Or only silence
when your name is spoken for the very last time.

*A line in a book and several old friends' new disease diagnoses prompted this.

SPECIAL BRANDS OF THE 'DÉJÀ VU'

Whenever I move to a new town
    I acquaint myself with the library first.
There is always at least one familiar book,
    Usually dog-eared and well-worn.

Paperweights in local antique shops I seek out.
    They are almost all like the one
Grandmother kept in that tall Cherrywood cupboard.
    It was a snowman with real snow.

And long walks in the evening, no matter where,
    always turn up at least one calico cat.
Who, if not exactly like my "Suliman,"
    is friendly, nonetheless.

A crumpled animal, thrown to the side of the road by
  a speeding car
    is too familiar. I've seen that form before,
that possum, that small dog, that broken fawn.
    For years I stopped and buried them.

Cemeteries, always quiet. Pioneer or physicist
    lying on hillsides catching the sunset's rays
spin universal yarns of human themes.
    All too often they lie forgotten, neglected.

Duane A. Partain

A green sweater found lying at the bottom of a trunk,
  mothballed
    since that hasty retreat from one too many episodes
of significant other closeness gone bad.
    The last time I called, she had moved.

A Ford Crown Victoria, mine was blue and white,
    had great pipes but used much oil.
I see them a lot on the streets now that I've past fifty.
    At least I think I do.

Old blues records recall many lonesome nights
    upstairs in a red brick corner building
listening to a cappella sounds
    only reflected neon lights for company.

Still, all remembrances are friends, of one sort or another.
    All memories evoke pleasant thoughts, at least a few,
and all should certainly be treasured phenomena
    as special brands of the 'Déjà vu.'

Many places, many people, many objects, many sights, many feelings—all become parts of our lives, if only for brief moments.

www.ingramcontent.com/pod-product-compliance
Lightning Source LLC
LaVergne TN
LVHW092051060526
838201LV00047B/1346